A Short History of Tyneham

by
BRIAN LEIGHTON JP

A SHORT HISTORY OF TYNEHAM

by

Brian Leighton JP

———

INTRODUCTION

Today it is difficult to recapture in the mind's eye the tranquil serenity of Tyneham Village as it was until the moment of military occupation in 1940 when the steady momentum of life of this flourishing rural community came to an end. Inevitably there is a touch of sadness which overshadows this former homely scene. Prior to World War II Tyneham was described as one of the most beautifully situated villages - an Elizabethan manor house, a few greystone cottages, a Church and School hidden among the trees with a distant vista of sea in a gap between towering hills and wide expanses of open grassland as one approaches from landward.

The one time rectory and street of cottages are now derelict and partially in ruin, many having become so dangerous that it has been necessary to remove their upper storeys and to cap their walls, leaving a ghost resemblance of the former village. Tyneham Church, now repaired by the military authorities, has become a centre of interest to visitors who seek to discover something of what the village was like in days gone by, and to acquaint themselves with the great variety of wild life which, after the exclusion of the public for some 34 years, still thrives, as in its unoccupied days, on heathland and in bog, on grassland and in woodland, on seashore, cliff and in stream.

Tyneham House was of considerable antiquarian interest and many regard its demolition, a few years ago, as an avoidable tragedy. Whilst subsequently to allow certain of its historic features, which were removed, to be incorporated in buildings elsewhere is regarded as an even more questionable decision.

However, it is pleasant to record that the Commandant of Lulworth Ranges and his senior staff, together with many of the Wardens, are vigilant and unceasing in their efforts to protect the many remaining antiquities and the rich variety of flora and fauna contained within this vast expanse of countryside, including some of Britain's rarer specimens.

The unique character of the Isle of Purbeck, and especially this western extremity, is accounted for by the fact that it was once a favourite hunting ground of Saxon and Norman Kings and, in consequence, remained undeveloped. The great family estates which succeeded ownership by the Crown have remained largely intact and now, given statutory protection, perpetuate the region of bold landscape, rugged coast and unique geological formation resulting from stresses in the earth's crust in the remote past.

CHAPTER 1

EARLY HABITATION

In and close to Tyneham there is prolific evidence of man's early occupancy of the soil.

Round Barrows

On Povington Heath there are 24 recorded Bronze Age Barrows. The Thorn Barrow group of six and its southern end is very close to the former village. Povington Barrow had a diameter of 56 feet and a height of 7 feet, which contained a Bronze Age Urn now in Dorset County Museum. Two large mounds have been found on Worbarrow Cliff, in one of them was discovered a Bronze Age Pin. To the WSW of Tyneham Church was a mound which contained seven human remains. Iron Age or later, in one was a small cup and a detached skull buried separately. Many of these barrows have been damaged, some by use as gunnery targets. Whilst there is plenty of evidence of Bronze Age burials in the Tyneham area there is no sign of where the people lived. One day a proper field survey may reveal the locality of these Bronze Age Settlements.

Celtic Fields

Celtic fields appear upon about 100 acres on the north slope of the west end of Purbeck Hills. In addition isolated and slight scarps occur on the corresponding south slope. Along the Tyneham coast north of Gold Down there are fragments of Celtic fields, mostly overlain by strip lynchets, some unusually irregular covering about five acres. These latter show up clearly when the sun is low in the sky and their particular interest is that strip fields cover them. Faint traces of other Celtic fields have been discovered at widely dispersed points.

Iron Age and Roman Finds

There is evidence of Iron Age occupation at Whiteway Farm. The pre-eminent example is at Flowers Barrow on Rings Hill, a pre-historic fort covering about 15 acres on the cliff edge of which probably a third has collapsed seaward as a result of erosion. There is evidence of quarrying of material to build ramparts, perhaps from the 4th century onwards resulting in a more elaborate structure than the original single fort. There are so many examples that one can only pick out a number of finds. Burials have been found near the head of Tyneham Gwyle about 150 ft above sea level, also bones, Samian ware and sherds (fragments of earthenware) and remains were found in a diverted stream bed. A human skeleton was unearthed in a nearby garden and others when removing the porch of St Mary's church. Seven interments and a separate buried skull were found in the rectory, one with a vessel near the head. At Worbarrow Bay habitation burials and occupation debris - perhaps of Iron Age or later Roman - have been found with evidence of shale working and perhaps salt industry. Near the cliff edge were revealed lumps of stone, including Purbeck marble acting as if the foundation for a floor. Below was charcoal, pottery, sling stones, spindle whorls of shale, bronze plaque. There too flint flakes with worn points, a fragment of an armlet, an iron knife and arrow head. Amongst these debris was a stone handmill, loom weight and a coin of Commodus. Nearby flanged bowls of 3rd or 4th century and colour coated pottery of this date from a site some 250 yards distant. An urn filled with what looked like black coins were identified as centres when cutting rings for personal ornaments.

Again there is plenty of evidence of Iron Age and Roman occupation and we can presume that from the 5th century BC onwards a pattern of farming was established in the valley and on the surrounding hills, a mixed economy of arable and pasture cultivated by individual farmers, growing corn, tending sheep, cattle and possibly pigs and using horses and dogs. Circular huts made up these farmsteads with pits where corn was dried and stored. The Roman administrators of the province no doubt exploited the inhabitants, but it is doubtful whether they persuaded them to change their Celtic methods of farming, so that the pattern established in the middle of the first millenium BC probably continued right up to the Colonisation of this area in the 7th century AD.

Saxon and Mediaeval Remains

The clear evidence of Saxon Estates forms a most impressive pattern hereabouts, for their boundaries are still marked by surviving continuous hedge lines which closely conform to the parish boundaries of today. In Tyneham Valley, in particular at Baltington and North Egliston, there are important earthwork remains of 13th century settlements which were once hamlets, and not just farms, for around both are earthworks which include the remains of house sites and gardens. All these sites are surrounded by a remarkable series of mediaeval arable cultivation strips, extending to a total of some 200 acres, which carefully respect the continuous hedge lines and nowhere cross them. South of the chalk ridge, mostly lynchets of contour type produced by mediaeval farmers ploughing across earlier Celtic fields, with traces of 18th century ploughing nearby.

Finally, it is salutary to reflect that but for the military presence modern deep ploughing methods could have obliterated substantial areas of these important prehistoric remains.

CHAPTER II

TYNEHAM PARISH

The parish, of some 3000 acres, lies five miles west of Corfe
Castle. It comprises a broad valley between the high ridges of
Gold Down and Tyneham Cap to the south and the bold Purbeck Hills
to the north which rise to over 600 feet. The southern ridge forms
the coastal cliff which, further to the east, rises to over 600
feet at Tyneham Cap; thereafter the land slopes down to Kimmeridge.
The valley is drained westward by a stream flowing through the
trees of the Gwyle into Worbarrow Bay. The name of Tyneham is
composed of two elements "Tyne", a river, and "ham" meaning a farm,
so perhaps Tyneham means "a farm by the river". The Oxford
Dictionary of English Place Names gives Tingeham Domesday Book,
Tigeham 1185, Tiham 1194 Pipe Rolls, Tynham 1280 Charter Rolls.
The Domesday Book records four adjoining areas called Tyneham,
which illustrates the care which the Conqueror took to reward his
followers in smallholdings, in order to prevent any one of them
obtaining a powerful local influence that might threaten the
central power. It seems evident that these today are probably
Tyneham itself, Baltington to the west and North Egliston (all in
the central valley) and South Egliston to the south of Tyneham Cap
- all four settlements were, it is said, in existence by the end of
the eleventh century. Slightly south of North Egliston is the site
of a Chapel of St Margaret.

To record the succession of titles over many centuries is
beyond the scope of this publication, but the area where the manor
house stood was probably held by Bretel, of Robert, Earl Mortain,
the Conqueror's half-brother. The second Tingeham was held by
William, of Hugh de Aberinas, Earl of Chester, son of the
Conqueror's sister, and before the Conquest, by a Saxon called
Alnod. The third Tingeham was held of the Queen by Anschitil
fitz-Amelene, and the fourth Tigeham was held by Edric, one of the
King's thegns styled "Eddricius praepositus".

Within the parish of Tyneham at the foot of this north side of
the Purbeck Hills is a series of small farms - a hamlet - known
collectively as Povington which anciently formed part of a larger
manor, held in demesne by Robert fitz-Gerald who was son of Gerald,
royal steward to King William I. Ancient chronicles record how the
Abbot of Bec (Duchy of Normandy) despite difficulties of laying
claim to English territory, succeeded in clinging to the good
things of the manor of Povington in the form of cheeses, oats, and
wool due to the Duchy in payment of rents. In a later period the
ownership of Povington, being in dispute, was decided by a trial by
wager of battle in which the Abbot won and the vanquished Knight
lost his claim.

All these parcels of land are rectangular in shape, their boundaries well defined with the existing lines which run across the area from one ridge to the other. In each of these areas totalling some 20 acres, are extensive and well preserved remains of cultivated strips which follow the continuous hedge lines and nowhere cross them. These appear in a regular manner with parallel base lines 20-40 yards apart up and down the slopes. These are marked by slight banks, or lynchets, about one foot high, in places running unbroken for at least 170 yards. Traces of irregular fields are clearer further east of Povington, extending over 25 acres.

In the Domesday Book Povington is recorded as a manor of eight and a half hides* worked by eight serfs with four villeins and five bordars as tenants; thus there is evidence that these four farms were already in existence in 1086. Up to the nineteenth century there was one large farm with just over 230 acres of land, four small farms each with between forty and seventy acres and eight or nine smallholdings each with a cottage and from five to fifteen acres of land. Professor Hoskins has pointed out that in all probability the large farm was the demesne of the Domesday Book and that the four small farms were the holdings of the four villeins recorded there. It is possible that some of these small holdings are those of the bordars.

It is not easy to identify the line of successive ownership of all these five portions of Tyneham, but as the largest and most important is the one containing the Church and Manor House, we will focus our search on this area. From the distant time when it probably belonged to Earl Mortain there is little reliable evidence until the reign of Queen Elizabeth I. It seems reasonable to suppose that the family of de Tyneham held the land here in early times. A manuscript in the British Library shows that Thomas Bardolph owned the manor and gave it to his daughter Rohesia upon her marriage to John Russell in 1202. John Russell had two sons, Ralph and Thomas; the former became the ancestor of the Duke of Bedford, and Thomas, it is believed, inherited Tyneham.

The Russells lived quietly at Tyneham for about a hundred years, the estate passing in direct line from father to son, but John Russell, fifth descendant from Thomas, died before his father and as he had no male issue the estate was divided between his four sisters. Johanna, the eldest, who had married Thomas Chyke, received the greater portion and thus the Chykes remained in possession of Tyneham for several generations and in the reign of Henry VIII, the property passed to John Pope in the right of his

---

* A mediaeval unit of land sufficient to maintain a household

wife Johanna who was heiress of the Chykes. John and Johanna Pope
sold the estate in 1523 to John Williams for life and that of his
second son Henry. It was Henry Williams who built the West wing of
the former mediaeval manor house.

Henry Williams, who survived his father, purchased the
reversion in 1563 from Thomas (son of John and Johanna) and when he
died in 1589 he was probably seized of the manor. John Williams
succeeded Henry and Jane, his only daughter, married Sir Robert
Lawrence of Grange who, in 1683, sold the manors of Tyneham and
Egliston to Nathaniel Bond of Lutton, whose family had settled
there in 1443. From thence, the property descended to Margaret
Sophia Bond, who on her marriage to Rev. Mathew Rogers, gave it to
her brother Rev. William Bond, rector of Tyneham, from whom it was
passed by succession to William Henry Bond and thence to his son,
the last owner, W.R.G. Bond who was obliged to leave his property
when it was compulsorily evacuated for military training by the
then War Office in 1943, and later relinquished it by compulsory
purchase in 1952. The letter ordering the evacuation in 1943 of
the whole of the Tyneham valley "within 28 days and for the
duration of the Emergency" was received by W.R.G. Bond by the same
post as a telegram reporting that his son was "missing in action"
in Italy. His son, later Major General H.M.G. Bond, JP, DL, now
lives near Dorchester and is a frequent visitor to Tyneham. He
planted the Silver Jubilee Oak near the car park by invitation of
the Army.

CHAPTER III

THE VILLAGE

In recalling the scenes of village life at the turn of the
century we can do no better than to draw upon the recollections of
Mrs L.M.G. Bond. Anyone who is interested enough to wish to learn
more about Tyneham, the central character in these few pages, is
advised to obtain a copy of her book "Tyneham" obtainable at the
Dorset County Museum.

The seemly row of houses which formed the street afforded a
good example of cottages built in local stone, their former thatch
having been replaced by stone slates about 1880, which blended with
mortared cottage walls of roughly dressed stone. The pond at the
southern end of the village was a favourite watering place for the
horses returning from a day's work to the farm. It was also
reputed to be a good place for eels - highly regarded as bait - and
it was the villagers' habit to sink hazel faggots into the pond for
a few days and then swiftly hoist them out together with the eels
which had crept into them. Henry Miller, the fisherman, would
carry them in his hat which he then replaced upon his head! The
southernmost cottage in the road was, by tradition, occupied by a

shepherd whose wife in latter days voluntarily performed the duties of the district nurse.

The next cottage was the post office combined with the village shop. These premises were tiny with a five foot counter which served both the office and the shop, the window space and walls were crammed with wares, while heavier articles, such as bags of flour and soda, stood on the floor. The counter piled high with parcels awaiting the postman, almost masked the post-mistress from her customers. A large box displayed a wide range of household articles such as needles, cotton, buttons and tape, pens, shoe-laces, matches and lozenges. The corners were crowded with many items such as candles, seeds etc. and overall hung a fine blend of odours dominated by the pungency of bacon and cheese. The telephone for receipt and despatch of telegrams only, was in the kitchen for the sake of privacy but much of what was said was audible to customers in the shop! Mrs Driscoll was the last of the postmistresses. Only in latter years did a carrier serve the village, previously goods were transported by farm wagon. The cottage next door to the post office went with the farm and housed successive carters and labourers.

The street curved round the School house garden on into the School yard, and on the west side were the ancient rectory cottages. In 1876 the parsonage was built, possessing a large sheltered garden producing prolific quantities of vegetables and bounded on one side by the churchyard. At the upper end of the village street a tap of spring water from Madmore stood back in a stone recess provided with a slab for the resting of pails while filling. An inscription thereon which reads "Whosoever drinketh of this water shall thirst again, but whosoever drinketh of the water that I shall give him shall never thirst". An oak, planted in 1910 to commemorate the Coronation of King George V, stands beside the stone recess.

No communal meeting place existed until 1926, when a Village Hall was built, after many years of money-raising effort. The Hall could accommodate the whole community, but sadly, in December 1929, the building was completely wrecked in a violent gale and it was years before a successor rose upon the site.

At the southern end of the village was Tyneham Farm. It was arranged in a series of closed-in yards, the rickyard, the stableyard and cowyard, with the carthorse stables and great barn on its further side, with a granary above, reached by an outside stone staircase. The barn was occasionally used for plays and pantomimes when raising funds to build the Village Hall, a rough stage being erected in the northern bay, the audience being accommodated in the south bay which could seat about 160 people comfortably. At Christmas, Mummers staged their traditional

8

performance, the words passing on verbally from one generation to another. Outdoor games, such as cricket and football, could not be played due to a lack of sufficient level ground. Within an area of some 3000 acres, the chief crops were barley, wheat and oats, together with some very good pasture.

Living conditions were severe for many, material comforts often primitive, yet undoubtedly there was a fine corporate spirit between friends and neighbours which helped to ease the privations and lack of amenities.

CHAPTER IV

THE CHURCH

The parish of Tyneham, originally in Bristol Diocese, but since 1836 in the Diocese of Salisbury, is dominated by the Church of St Mary the Virgin, standing on high ground above the curve of the village street. Mediaeval in origin and cruciform in plan, the architecture of Early English and Decorated styles, the Church contains, in the North transept, a piscina dating back to 1300. The fabric, including rebuilding of the west wall, was restored in 1744. When the seating of the Church became inadequate, the South transept was built by the Rev. William Bond and the North transept, which had been used by the family, was given over to the congregation, the seats becoming rudely known as "the Cowstalls". Under the direction of the architect Benjamin Ferrey, the former south porch, circa 14th century, was dismantled and rebuilt as the west porch in 1880.

The North transept was a chantry chapel belonging to the manor; indeed, it is probable that the church originated as the chapel of the great house. In the North transept there is a monument to John Williams 1627 (who succeeded Henry Williams) and to his wife 1636 erected by their grandson John Williams in 1641 which asserts that buried underneath are the bones of Henry of Tyneham, son of John Williams. Also in the North transept there is a plain cross inscribed I.H.S. ORATE PRO NOBIS.

The roof of the church is covered with stone slates except the nave which was originally covered in lead. The lead was stolen soon after the evacuation of the village and was replaced by a bituminous material. This part of the roof has now been tiled by the Army.

There is a bellcote in which were hung two bells, one inscribed "in nomine domini", cast in Salisbury circa 1500, and the second by R. Wells, Aldborne 1784, one bell is now stored in Steeple Church and one hung at West Parley. The bell ropes passed through lead guides and the ringer stood on the chancel steps, the choir having to dodge the ropes in order to reach their places.

The three-sided Jacobean pulpit is on loan to Lulworth Camp. There are monuments in Caen stone in memory of the distinguished members of the Bond family, and in the nave there is a touching record of a faithful servant, who is remembered in a stone tablet to Elizabeth Tarrant, servant of Mrs Bond, in which station she continued 34 years, in recognition of her prudence, honesty and industry. She died August 2nd 1769 in her 54th year. A further tablet commemorates the devoted service of Hannah Hunworth, nurse to the Bond family for many years. An Elizabethan chalice and pattern by Louis Stratford, Dublin, c. 1570 remains in safe keeping. The sanctuary contains a lancet window in remembrance of Nathaniel Bond. Early this century a beautiful east window, made by Martin Travers, was donated in memory of Mrs Draper of Worbarrow. The window represents the Madonna and Child under a growing tree and has three lights - on either side are panels, designed by Christopher Draper, depicting Tyneham life, showing a labourer busy with his plough and fishermen putting out to sea with their boat. By agreement with Philip Draper, her elder son, this window is to be replaced.

The interior of the building, recently whitened, has lost its enchanting aroma of an old village church, which is a blend of leather bindings, old music, straw hassocks, candle-wax and lamp oil. Heating, we are told, was by a "Tortoise" stove installed at the crossing and together with the oil lamps kept the congregation snug on Sunday evenings. A homely feature was a gallery at the west end with a row of hat pegs underneath. The gallery was generally used by the shy male parishioners. The chancel held a remarkably fine pipe organ given as a thanks offering for the safe homecoming of Captain Algernon Bond who, severely wounded, survived the Siege of Ladysmith, and whose memorial window has been re-erected in the South transept. This organ has now been installed in Steeple church. Previously music was provided by a barrel organ which played the metrical psalms, and later by a harmonium which, because of the damp, was transported to and from the church on Sundays.

The Registers, dating from 1694, are deposited in the Dorset Record Office, County Hall, Dorchester. A mystery surrounds the identity of seafarers who lie buried in the churchyard sheltered by the chancel wall.

Divine services in this church formerly took place once each Sunday and at festivals, but in 1848 the Rev. W. Bond donated a capital sum of £1700 to Queen Anne's Bounty on condition that the rector performed two services with a sermon every Sunday, on Good Friday and at Christmas. The living was annexed to Steeple with the residence (now demolished) and twenty acres of glebeland all of which were in Tyneham. The living was held, at the time of requisition, by the Rev. H.C. Money. With Tyneham linked in this way to Steeple parish, it is interesting to recall that the Washington Arms, more widely known as "the stars and stripes" are emblazoned on the barrel roof of Steeple church - long before the American flag was thought of. The squires of Steeple, the Lawrences, were allied to the ancestors of George Washington and it was in 1616 that the arms of Sir Oliver Lawrence were inscribed in a panel over the door of the church of "St Mycheal" at Steeple.

From the list of Rectors of Tyneham, which appears in the Appendix, it will be noted the length of incumbency in four instances must be nearly a record embracing spans of 44 to 53 years!

CHAPTER V

THE SCHOOL

The School was built on glebeland in 1860 by the Rector, Rev. Nathaniel Bond, from materials of an old Tithe Barn, at his own expense. It was composed of a single large room (28' x 15') with a lobby at one end and a narrow platform at the other for infants' benches and/or use as an improvised stage. The building remained private property and was managed by the Rector and his Curate (Rev. William Freck), the income of £38.5.0 being derived from Voluntary Subscriptions (£31.5.0) and School pence (£7.0.0) paid weekly by children in attendance. The records of 1871 indicate that the school employed a teacher named James Roe, with one lady assistant. This full range pupil school was intended for up to 60 children and remained in use until 1932 when it was closed owing to the small number of scholars; Miss L. Hearne being the last mistress. The School occupied the land in the Street and was connected to the School-house by its garden. An unusual feature is that the stone roof is now largely covered by ferns. As Tyneham Church had neither tower nor spire the parish flagstaff stood in the grounds, safe from cattle, and flew its flag on occasions of national and local rejoicing.

It is recorded that the teachers cared deeply for the moral and physical welfare of their charges, instilling high ideals and standards of behaviour and providing a solid grounding in essentials. Many acts of kindness found expression such as the provision of hot potatoes to accompany the children's dinners, or discreet assistance with boots and clothing when poorer mothers were in difficulties, and the provision of warm slippers for use in school, while garments were dried out on the central stove. Many entertainments took place on the narrow platform — the unwieldy forms being removed from the body of the School and stacked outside, each household lending chairs for the use of the audiences. Whether these performances were of high thespian standard or not, they varied in their content and ingenuity, to the tumultuous delight of the village community. The School also served as a reading room and on winter nights the lads could play table games.

CHAPTER VI

THE MANOR HOUSE

This ancient house, recently demolished, was built by Henry Williams — it was commenced in 1567 and completed in 1583 as the date and his initials inscribed on a small shield over the original east doorway. The main building was of two storeys, part with attic and cellars built mainly in Purbeck ashlar, quarried on the estate. This fine specimen of Tudor architecture included three gables and a centre porch. At an earlier period — date unrecorded — there was a courtyard with a gatehouse, the foundations of which could be discerned in the turf of the lawn in hot dry seasons. The upper windows were of three lights with stone mullions and surrounds; those of the ground floor were replaced in 1820 with hung sashes when other alterations took place. Thomas Bond, a well-known antiquarian, inserted in the north wall of the library an exact replica of the original mullioned windows which were sacrificed in the interests of light and air. The composition of the house was quiet and unpretentious and had mellowed over the 350 years of its life. When the house was finally acquired by the War Office, the 17th century panelling, a fine wood overmantel and some ancient glass were removed to Dorset County Museum, where they were received as a memorial to the last owner, Ralph Bond, who was at the time of his death President of the Dorset Natural History and Archaeological Society.

On the south west side of the main building are the remains of the 14th century house (still in existence though at present out of bounds), which rival the oldest parts of Barnston Manor. The original structure, built by Russell, is known to have contained a hall 36 ft x 20 ft. When this was no longer required the hall was divided by a crosswall and chimney stack, the arch of the massive open fire being circa 16th century. Its brick oven, still intact, was in use for baking bread until the turn of the century. A floor was inserted dividing the area into two storeys, the thick walls were pierced for the insertion of windows and a winding stone stair built to connect the two floors. This building in the 1890s was occupied by the dairyman.

A portion of the mediaeval timbered roof trusses supported by hammer beams remains, but now incongruously sheeted with corrugated iron. This replaces the stone slates which were considered by the Ancient Monuments division of the Ministry of Works (as it then was) to be too heavy and likely to precipitate the collapse of this fine specimen of early timber roofing. The building came to be known as the "Old House" and it is deeply to be regretted that a mediaeval lintel and stone surround have been removed. If it is not too late to salvage, these undoubted antiquities, together with the stone tiles of the roof, should be preserved against the day when this building can be expertly restored and opened to the discerning antiquarian.

There are the remains of some outlying properties at South Egliston. Hidden in the trees is an 18th century two storey house with stone mullioned windows, altered in the 19th century by the provision of French windows and a loggia and, nearby, an 18th century cottage of one storey with an attic above.

The house was a popular holiday retreat for members of the Bond family and their friends and a path through a coppice led down from this house to Broad Bench, a wide expanse of flat rock where, at low tide, games were played and picnic parties held. The writer well recalls the pungent odour of wild garlic in this narrow strip of woodland.

CHAPTER VII

WORBARROW BAY

Worbarrow Bay was the site of a hamlet of fishermen's cottages and the homes of coastguards. Here the sea has cut through the valley to expose the geological formation of the earth's strata. The coastguard's lookout, flagstaff and signal cannon were sited on the Tout, a limestone conical-shaped hill protruding into the sea, almost surrounded by water and joined to the mainland cliff by a thin neck of land. The coastguard station itself and cottages stood behind the stone slipway, the remains of which can still be seen. From the Tout there is an unobstructed view up and down the coast. To the west lies the narrow ravine called Arish Mell and beyond this Mupe Bay and Mupe Rocks. Further to the west is the great mass of Bindon Hill, the western extremity of Purbeck, and in the far distance the Isle of Portland, with its naval harbour.

To the east lies the rocky Pondfields cove and Gold Down with its magnificent Gad Cliff and a panoramic view of some of the finest scenery in the South of England. In the far distance, on a clear day, can be seen St Aldhelm's Head, nearer lies the deep

13

inlet of Chapman's Pool and closer still Kimmeridge Bay, with Clavell's Tower on the headland above, while in the middle distance Broad Bench stretches far out into the surf. Just east of Broad Bench lies Brandy Bay, so called because the nooks and crannies of its surrounding rocks were once used by smugglers as a hiding place for their contraband. Tales are told of the way in which flocks of sheep were driven to and fro along the cliff tops to obliterate the signs of horse and cart and winch and tackle whereby the smugglers hoisted and removed their goods from the beach far below.

Gad Cliff overhangs the sea to a height of over 400 ft, a sanctuary for rare birds such as the raven and peregrine, whilst right below is a small cave, dangerous to reach, accessible only at certain tides, which was also used for smuggling.

The fishermen of Worbarrow, all named Miller, were tough seamen, gentle and honest in character, and much loved by the regular summer visitors, many of whom lodged with Jack and Alice Miller in their cottage on the beach. In their young days this remarkable couple met as coachman and cook at an hotel in Swanage. Privileged visitors were treated to expertly cooked four or six course dinners all performed on a two burner cooker. The other Millers were also very friendly though rather shy of strangers and they could tell good yarns of the days of smuggling around their coast. They were all indeed a worthy breed and were known and appreciated throughout Dorset. The coastguard families, mostly retired R.N. Servicemen, kept the place alive in Victorian times, but their station was disbanded in about 1910. The coastal footpath was well defined by the daily patrols of the Coastguards and was marked by whitened stones every few yards as a guide at night or in fog. Sadly, these stones have been all thrown over the cliff by playful visitors.

CONCLUSION

Thus we must conclude our brief story. Despite the tragic loss of the ancient manor house at Tyneham and the advanced decay of former picturesque cottages, there remains a strong sense of historic continuity which exerts an irrisistible appeal to a great number of people who are fascinated by the long record of archaeological remains, and are eager to explore a remote area of countryside which few counties can match, encompassed by the Tyneham Ranges. In equity, we must acknowledge the parts played by the Army in its protective role and the Dorset County Council in signposting the walks.

Those who knew the freedom of the valley in the days before the military occupation may well have strongly resented the continued Army presence after the war was over. Indeed, there were many efforts made and campaigns launched to persuade the military to vacate Tyneham: but this was not to be and, with the passing of the years, the status quo has become accepted and today the military authorities can be regarded as partners in the protection, preservation and unobtrusive control of this lovely corner of Purbeck, quiet, peaceful unsurpassed for its natural beauty and historic atmosphere, and now, thankfully, available once more at most weekends and holidays for the enjoyment of all who cherish our countryside.

Instituted:

1304	William de Cane
1313	John de Clenche
1349	John West
1350	John Colart
1391	Richard Heryng
1415	Richard Beake
1440	Richard Holdeche
1447	John Courtellir
1451	Thomas Benet
1453	John Somersed
1457	William Burgney
1464	William Buckhorne
1466	John Aldeston
1468	John Martyn
1471	Thomas Mone
1488	John Bryan
	Richard Whittock
1507	Robert Bremmer
1510	John Pope
1530	Edward Kyxley MA
1538	Adam Rickeman
1582	Humphrey Fletcher
1595	Henry Russel
1617	Joseph Dyke MA
1663	Joseph Tomes MA
1681	John Riccard BA
1692	Bernard Toup BA
1722	Samuel Bolde
1738	Christopher Twiniho MA
	(After this was united with Steeple)
1742	Denis Bond MA
1795	William Bond BA
1852	Nathaniel Bond BA
1889	Christopher Wordsworth MA
1897	Claude Samual Homan BA
1914	Edward Clifford Howther MA
1916	Thomas Openshaw Coupe MA
1923	Frederick de la Poer Beresford Corfield
1927	Christopher Campbell Sharpe MA
1933	Edwin George Clifford Frend BA
1937	Humphrey Churchill Money

BIBLIOGRAPHY

L.M.G. Bond	"Tyneham"	1956
J. Hutchins	"The History and Antiquities of Dorset" 3rd Edition	1861–1870
Ida Woodward	"In and Around the Isle of Purbeck"	1907
Christopher Taylor	"The Making of the English Landscape: Dorset	1970
C.E. Robinson	"A Royal Warren"	1882
	Royal Commission on Historical Monuments Vol II South East Dorset Part 2	1970

ACKNOWLEDGMENTS

Miss Margaret Holmes MA   County Archivist Dorset

R.N.R. Peers MA, FSA, FMA   Curator, Dorset County Museum

Philip Draper C.Eng

Alan M. Barker   Diocesan Registrar Salisbury

Donald Gain FIOB

All nett proceeds from the sale of this booklet will be used for the protection of the environment and towards the cost of amenities for the visiting public.